What Are Crystals?

Molly Aloian

Crabtree Publishing Company

www.crabtreebooks.com

Crabtree Publishing Company

www.crabtreebooks.com

Author: Molly Aloian

Publishing plan research and development:
Sean Charlebois, Reagan Miller
Crabtree Publishing Company

Project coordinator: Kathy Middleton

Photo research: Tibor Choleva, Melissa McClellan

Design: Tibor Choleva

Editor: Adrianna Morganelli

Proofreaders: Rachel Stuckey, Crystal Sikkens

Production coordinator: Margaret Amy Salter

Prepress technician: Margaret Amy Salter

Print coordinator: Katherine Berti

Geological consultant:

David G. Morse, PhD, Prairie Research Institute,
University of Illinois Urbana-Champaign, Illinois

Cover: Spa salt (center); amethyst crystal (bottom right); blue quartz crystal (bottom left); silica quartz crystal (bottom middle)

Title page: Gypsum crystals geode from Herja Mine

Special thanks: Jyoti Nagpal

This book was produced for Crabtree Publishing Company by BlueAppleWorks.

Photographs and reproductions:

© dreamstime.com: Kaarsten(headline and boxtop image), Giuliachristin(4 large), Grafvision (4 left), Byelikova(5 top), Pancaketom(5 middle), Fireflyphoto(5 bottom), Viktarm(7 middle), Gyeah(7 top), Pretoperola(8 top), Natis76(10/11 large), Rainer Walter Schmied(11 bottom right, 15 middle center, 26 top), Scrambled (14 left), Michal Baranski(14 top right), Gozzoli(15 top), Gabriel Robledo(15 middle left), Zelenka68(15 middle right, 29 large), Irina Beloturova (15 bottom), Danolsen(16 bottom left), Dan Wallace(18/19 large), Nguyen Thai(18 top), Vinicius Tupinamba(18 middle), Martin Novak(18 bottom), Saraizzo(19 bottom), Vallefrias (20/21 large), Gozzoli(21{8},29, 2cd from top), Farbled(21{9}, 29, 2cd from bottom), Ramunas Bruzas(23 middle), Matthew Weinel(24/25 large), Vladimirdavydov(7 bottom, 29, 3rd from bottom), Digitalpress(26/27 large, 28 bottom), Allocricetulus(26 bottom), Gozzoli(27 top), Alexandar Iotzov(27 middle), Allocricetulus(28 top), Ileanaolaru(28, 2cd from top), Alexander Maksimov(28 middle), Valentyn75(29 top), Ellione(29 bottom) / © iStockphoto.com: Florea Marius Catalin(10 left), Melissa Carroll(16/17 large), Mlenny Photography(25 top), oonal(27 bottom) / © Shutterstock.com: Gontar(cover: bottom middle), Bart_J(cover: bottom left), Dja65(cover: bottom right), Subbotina Anna(cover center), Presniakov Oleksandr(background every page) iliuta goean(titlepage, 9 left), Luca Moi(5 large), Mirka Moksha(4 right), Anton Balazh(6/7 large), hjschneider(6 right), Lukiyanova Natalia/frenta(6 bottom), Tyler Boyes(8 middle, 21{5},21{6}), Tom Grundy(9 right), AridOcean(9 bottom, 13 middle), Gala_Kan(10 right), Madlen(11 top), Manamana(11 right middle and bottom middle, 25 left), Only Fabrizio (11 bottom left), Tatiana Grozetskaya(12/13 large), AptTone(12 bottom), teena137(12 top), AVprophoto(13 top), Christopher Kolaczan(13 bottom), Johannes Kornelius(14 bottom right), Karol Kozlowski(17 top), nadi555(17 middle), Kompaniets Taras(17 bottom), botaz-solti(20 top), mehmetcan(20 bottom), lightpoet(21 top), vikiri(21 middle), Terry Davis(21{2}, 25 right), Jiri Slama(21{3}), Nicholas Sutcliffe(21{4}), Fribus Ekaterina(21{7}), MarcelClemens(21{10}), Alexander Hoffmann(24 top), URRRA(25 middle), wanchai(25 bottom), AptTone(28, 2cd from bottom), Nadezda Boltaca(29, 3rd from top), Amikphoto(29 middle) / © Thinkstock: iStockphoto(8 bottom, 14/15 large), Stockbyte(8/9 large) Science Photo Library: © Javier Trueba 22(both images), 23 top / public domain: 21{1} / © Kerstin Langenberger 23 bottom / Tectonic Map courtesy of the U.S. Geological Survey: 9 bottom

Library and Archives Canada Cataloguing in Publication

Aloian, Molly
        What are crystals? / Molly Aloian.

(Let's rock)
Includes index.
Issued also in electronic formats.
ISBN 978-0-7787-7213-2 (bound).--ISBN 978-0-7787-7218-7 (pbk.)

        1. Crystals--Juvenile literature. 2. Crystallography--Juvenile literature. I. Title. II. Series: Let's rock (St. Catharines, Ont.)

QD906.3.A46 2012   j549'.18   C2012-900254-2

Library of Congress Cataloging-in-Publication Data

CIP available at Library of Congress

Crabtree Publishing Company

www.crabtreebooks.com   1-800-387-7650

Printed in Canada/022012/AV20120110

Published in Canada
Crabtree Publishing
616 Welland Ave.
St. Catharines, Ontario
L2M 5V6

Published in the United States
Crabtree Publishing
PMB 59051
350 Fifth Avenue, 59th Floor
New York, New York 10118

Published in the United Kingdom
Crabtree Publishing
Maritime House
Basin Road North, Hove
BN41 1WR

Published in Australia
Crabtree Publishing
3 Charles Street
Coburg North
VIC 3058

CONTENTS

THE ORIGINS OF CRYSTALS

Crystals are all around you. They can be many different sizes, colors, and shapes, but they are always solids. Crystals have flat sides, angled edges, and sharp corners. Crystals that are cut and polished are often called **gems**.

MADE OF MINERALS

A crystal is made of an individual **mineral** with a specific chemical formula and arrangement of atoms. All rocks are made up of minerals. There are thousands of different minerals on Earth. Minerals can form as crystals. For example, table salt is composed of the mineral called halite. Salt grains are composed of individual crystal fragments. Rocks that are inside Earth are made up of minerals and virtually all of these minerals are made up of crystals. Quartz, gold, and salt are examples of minerals that can be found in rocks.

▶ Salt crystals line the rocks and cliffs around the Dead Sea in Jordan.

NAME GAME

✳ The word "crystal" comes from the Greek word *krystallos*, which is derived from the word *kryos*. *Kryos* means "icy cold" in Greek. Long ago, people believed that rock crystal was ice that had frozen so hard it would never melt. Rock crystal is a type of quartz.

▼ Rock crystal is a pure, colorless form of quartz.

4

CRYSTAL EARTH

There are crystals in many places on Earth. Some crystals form in caves deep underground. Others form inside stones or on the ocean floors. Ice is a crystal made of water. When ice melts and turns into liquid, it is no longer a crystal.

THE CRYSTALS IN THE GRANITE

Parts of Earth's **crust** are made up of a type of rock called granite. Granite consists mainly of quartz, feldspar, and mica, which are all minerals. There are many crystals of these minerals in granite.

▲ Sulfur crystals are formed by volcanic gases on the sides of volcanic craters.

▲ The crystals in granite can be easily seen.

▼ The Yosemite National Park, in California, is well known for its massive granite cliffs.

MADE OF CRYSTALS

✳ Most non-living substances are made up of crystals.

◄ Flakes of gold may be composed of hundreds or thousands of crystals of gold.

EARTH LAYERS

Earth is made up of different layers of rock. The outermost layer of Earth is called the crust. Below the crust is the **mantle**, which is a very thick, dense layer of rock. These layers are made of solid, rock-forming minerals that form crystals.

HOT STUFF

The mantle is approximately 1,800 miles (2,897 km) thick—much thicker than the crust. The outer core is the next layer. The temperature of the outer core is very hot, but the inner core is even hotter. The temperature of the inner core is about 9,000°F (4,982°C).

MAGNETIC ROCK

✳ Crystals in magnetite, a mineral in basalt, act like tiny compass needles lining up with Earth's magnetic field. Scientists use magnetite to study the movements of **tectonic plates**.

▼ *A sample of magnetite*

crust

mantle

inner core

outer core

THE CORE OF THE MATTER

(This activity needs adult supervision.)

This experiment will give you an idea of what Earth's layers look like.

You will need:

- a hardboiled egg or an avocado
- a knife

Cut the hardboiled egg or avocado in half. Imagine that the egg yolk or avocado pit is the layers of Earth's core. The egg white or the green flesh is the mantle. Imagine that the egg shell or the avocado skin is the crust.

▲ A map of the boundaries of the tectonic plates

SUPERCONTINENT

✳ Hundreds of millions of years ago, there was only one continent on Earth. It was a supercontinent called Pangaea.

▼ All Earth's continents were once combined to form Pangaea.

◀ An avocado, when cut in half, resembles the structure of Earth.

MOVING PLATES

Earth's crust is divided into giant slabs of rock called tectonic plates. These plates do not stay in the same place. They are constantly moving, which causes earthquakes and volcanic eruptions on Earth. Tectonic plates move very slowly, but the changes on Earth can be enormous. The island called Iceland formed when two plates moved apart and **magma** rose up to fill in the gap.

HOW DO CRYSTALS FORM?

Most of the crystals on Earth were formed millions of years ago. Most crystals form when hot molten, or liquid, rock from inside Earth cools and hardens. If the molten rock cools quickly, the crystals that form are tiny. If the rock cools slowly, the crystals may get very large.

DIFFERENT TYPES

There are different types of rocks on Earth. Igneous rocks form when magma cools and hardens. Metamorphic rocks are formed by heat and pressure in Earth's crust. Changes in heat and pressure cause minerals to change their form and size. For example, granite can change into gneiss and the crystals within it change, too. Sedimentary rocks are made out of **sediment**. Sedimentary rock can contain tiny pieces of crystal.

▲ Pegmatite is an igneous rock composed of large crystals.

▼ Basalt is an igneous rock composed of small crystals.

▼ Crystals in gneiss form wavy bands.

CRYSTALS IN IGNEOUS ROCKS

The size of the crystals in igneous rocks usually indicates where the rock formed. Crystals in igneous rocks formed below Earth's surface tend to be large because the magma takes longer to cool. Smaller crystals usually form above Earth's surface because it is cooler. This happens when volcanoes erupt and shoot out **lava**. The lava hardens into igneous rock and crystals form quickly.

▲ *Gypsum crystals are usually white, colorless, or gray.*

IN SHAPE

✱ Crystals can form in many different shapes. For example, crystals of mica silicates are flat and thin. Thin gypsum crystals look like needles.

▲ *Mica is a group of silicates that **cleave** into flat sheets.*

VOLCANO!

Volcanoes usually occur in places where tectonic plates collide or spread apart. During a volcanic eruption, magma from inside Earth shoots out and runs down the side of the volcano. Many volcanic eruptions and earthquakes take place within an area called the Ring of Fire that borders the Pacific Ocean.

▶ *The Ring of Fire is an area where large numbers of earthquakes and volcanic eruptions occur.*

CRYSTAL SYSTEMS

Acrystal is a solid material. A crystal's atoms and molecules are arranged in a pattern. This pattern is repeated over and over throughout the whole crystal. The atoms are like tiny building blocks. A crystal is made up of millions of atoms that fit together in a special pattern to form the crystal.

SEVEN SYSTEMS

Crystals have been divided into seven types or categories based on different amounts of **symmetry**.

The categories are called systems. The seven systems are the cubic system, the trigonal system, the tetragonal system, the hexagonal system, the orthorhombic system, the monoclinic system, and the triclinic system.

ABOUT ATOMS

✳ An atom is the basic unit of matter. Atoms join other atoms in specific ways to create structures.

▶ A model of regularly spaced atoms that form the building block of a crystal

▼ Rock salt is a cubic type of crystal.

▼ Amazonite feldspar is a triclinic type of crystal.

ABOUT ATOMS

Crystals in the cubic system have the highest symmetry. Crystals in the triclinic system have the least symmetry.

SALT AND SUGAR

You will need:

- black paper
- salt
- sugar
- magnifying glass

Place a few grains of salt on the piece of black paper and look at them with the magnifying glass. What do you see? Place a few grains of sugar on the paper. Do they look the same as the salt crystals? How are they different?

▲ *Sugar is a monoclinic type of crystal.*

▼ *Zircon is a tetragonal type of crystal.*

FACE IT

✳ All crystals have a definite shape. They also have flat surfaces called **faces**. Faces meet at precise angles following the arrangement of the atoms.

▼ *Aquamarine is a hexagonal type of crystal.*

crystal face   crystal angle

▼ *Aragonite is an orthorhombic type of crystal.*

▼ *Calcite is a trigonal type of crystal.*

DIAMONDS

Most diamonds are formed deep within Earth's mantle. Diamond is made of pure carbon and is the hardest naturally occurring substance on Earth. Diamonds were first discovered over 2,000 years ago.

DIAMOND DEPOSITS

Diamonds are usually found in three types of deposits. They are found in materials, including silt, sand, and clay, deposited by rivers. They are found in the materials deposited by **glacial ice**. They are also found in kimberlite. Kimberlite is a type of volcanic rock that was first discovered in the Kimberley region of South Africa. Australia, Congo, Russia, and South Africa are among the top diamond-producing countries in the world.

▲ *Small amounts of impurities color diamonds blue, yellow, brown, green, purple, pink, orange, or red.*

TURNING COLOR

Colorless diamonds are made of pure carbon. Colored diamonds form when they contain small amounts of impurities such as boron for blue diamonds or nitrogen for yellow to brown diamonds.

▲ *Gem-quality diamonds are relatively rare. Most diamonds mined today are used for industrial purposes.*

DAZZLING DIAMOND

Rare and beautiful diamonds are very valuable and are worth millions of dollars. One of the largest diamonds ever found is called the Cullinan diamond. A miner named Thomas Evan Powell found the diamond in the Premiere Mine in South Africa. It weighed 3,106 carats (621 g).

GLEAMING SHEEN

✳ Diamonds mined from kimberlites often have **lustrous** crystal faces.

▼ Gem-quality diamonds are often very small.

◄ South Africa is one of the world's major gem-quality diamond producers.

◄ The Mir Mine is an open pit diamond mine in Russia. The mine is 1,722 feet (525 m) deep. It is the second largest excavated hole in the world.

▼ Diamonds in their natural rough and uncut form

QUARTZ

Quartz commonly forms crystals. Quartz is made of silicon dioxide and is the second most abundant mineral in Earth's crust. Quartz is sometimes found as individual crystals. It also occurs as large, fine-grained masses in a wide variety of forms, patterns, and colors.

USING QUARTZ

Quartz is found in almost all igneous, metamorphic, and sedimentary rocks. It is tough and highly resistant to weathering, so quartz sand can be used to make glass and **ceramics**. Crushed quartz is also used in sandpaper. Sandstone is made up mainly of quartz. It is an important building stone.

▼ *Pieces of quartz that have been crushed into sand are glued to a paper backing to make sandpaper.*

BIG ROCK!

✳ One of the largest rock crystals ever found was about 20 feet (six m) long and weighed more than 92,400 pounds (41,912 kg).

▼ *Sandstone is a common building and paving material.*

▼ *Quartz sand is a common raw material for the manufacture of some glasses and ceramics, such as porcelain.*

14

FANCY QUARTZ

The most common single crystals of quartz are clear rock crystal, purple amethyst, rose quartz, smoky quartz, and a yellow quartz called citrine. These crystals are often found in large pieces that can be cut as **gemstones**.

▲ *Clear quartz*

▼ *Rose quartz comes in shades of pink.*

▼ *Citrine is a yellowish variety of quartz.*

▼ *Smoky-colored quartz*

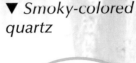

◄ *The transformation of raw materials (quartz sand) into glass takes place at around 2,400°F (1,315°C).*

▼ *Amethyst is the purple variety of the mineral quartz, and its most valuable and prized variety.*

SHINING COLORS!

Colorless rock crystal is the purest form of quartz. As in diamonds, other colors are caused by impurities. For example, there is iron in amethyst and citrine, and titanium and iron in rose quartz.

CORUNDUM

Corundum is made of aluminum oxide. Rubies and sapphires are varieties of this mineral. After diamonds, rubies and sapphires are the hardest natural substances on Earth. They are also valued gemstones. When iron and titanium are present in corundum, the mineral is called a blue sapphire. A small amount of chromium atoms turns corundum into a red ruby.

RUBIES AND SAPPHIRES

The Kashmir region of the Indian subcontinent is famous for its blue sapphires, which exhibit an intense, vivid shade of blue that came to be known as "Kashmir blue." Madagascar, Australia, and Sri Lanka also produce gem sapphires. Most of the highest quality rubies are mined in Myanmar. Rubies from the legendary mines in Mogok often have a bright red color. Rubies from Myanmar, Pakistan, and Afghanistan are often found in **marble**.

▼ Ruby is the red variety of corundum, the second-hardest natural mineral known to humankind.

ROCK HARD

Most corundum is not of gemstone quality, however. It is **opaque** and gray or brown. Because of its hardness, it is used in industrial **abrasives** to cut and polish softer materials.

▲ Corundum used for abrasives is mined in Zimbabwe, Russia, Sri Lanka, and India.

TRUE COLORS

✱ Corundum is a **pleochroic mineral**. Pleochroic minerals show different colors depending on the direction at which they are viewed.

◄ Natural ruby crystals are formed by intense heat and pressure.

▲ A high-quality ruby is often more valuable than a diamond of the same size.

▼ Sapphire is the most precious and valuable blue gemstone.

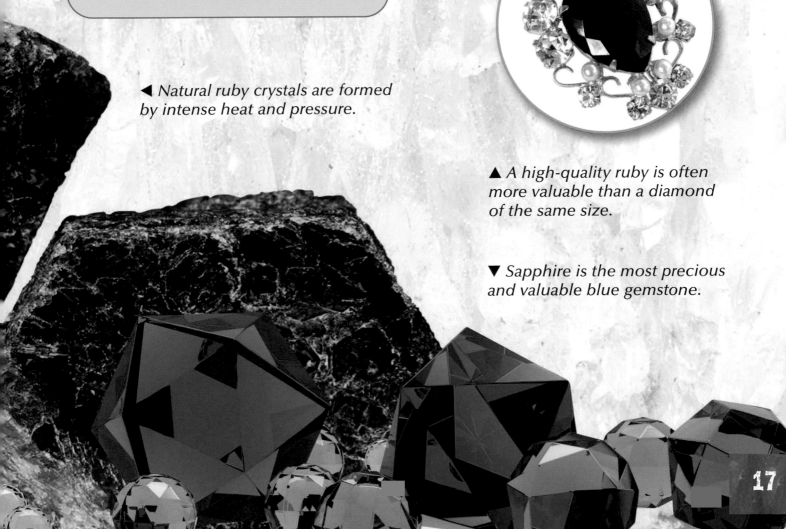

BERYL

Beryl is made up of beryllium aluminum silicate. It forms hexagonal crystals. Beryl is a popular gemstone because of its beautiful colors and resistance to wear. The most well known types of beryl gems are emeralds and aquamarines.

BLUE-GREEN AQUAMARINE

Pure beryl is colorless, but the mineral iron causes beautiful blues and yellows. Aquamarine ranges from pale green to blue, depending on the amounts of different forms of iron. Aquamarine is found in many countries, but the most is found in Brazil. One of the largest aquamarine gemstones came from the Papamel Mine in Brazil in 1910. It weighed over 240 pounds (109 kg) and was 19 inches (48 cm) long and 17 inches (43 cm) wide.

▲ *Deep green is the most desired color in emeralds.*

◀ *Aquamarine was named for the Latin phrase "water of the sea" because of its blue-green color.*

▲ *Light blue colored stones are the most common type of aquamarine.*

GOOD ENOUGH TO EAT!

(This activity needs adult supervision.)

Make your own candy crystals.

You will need:

- 1½ cups (355 ml) of sugar
- ½ cup (118 ml) of boiling water
- a spoon for stirring
- an empty cup
- food coloring
- a piece of string
- a pencil
- a paper clip

Boil the water in a pan. Using a potholder, remove the pan from the heat. Add the sugar to the water and stir until it is dissolved. Pour the solution into a cup. Stir in three drops of food coloring. Tie the paper clip to one end of the string and tie the pencil to the other end of the string. Place the pencil across the top of the cup so the string and paper clip dangle in the water. Set the cup aside for a few days. You'll soon have your very own sugar crystals to munch on!

▶ *Emerald is one of the most difficult gemstones to cut because it is very brittle.*

MINING EMERALDS

Some of the most rare and most spectacular emeralds in the world were found near Muzo and Chivor in Columbia. The Chibcha Indians of Columbia mined emeralds over 500 years ago. These emeralds were traded with other ancient civilizations in the Americas, including the Incas of Peru and the Aztecs of Mexico. Long ago, people also mined emeralds near the Red Sea in Egypt. Today, the most important mine in Columbia is the Coscuez Mine.

▼ *Inca traders used special trails to cross high stony mountain ranges.*

USING CRYSTALS

The most common use of crystals is in jewelry and other decorations, but certain crystals are also valuable for use in industry and medicine.

DOING IT WITH DIAMONDS

Diamonds with flaws or diamonds of poor color can still be used for their hardness. For example, manufacturers put whole diamonds into tools or bake crushed diamonds into cutting tools. People can then use these tools to cut and shape the metals used to make cars and other automobiles, airplanes, and other machinery. Diamonds are also used in saws and drill bits, clocks, and lasers.

TIPPED OFF

✳Diamond-tipped drills are used for drilling all types of rock because diamonds are so hard.

▼ Dentists use diamond-tipped drills, too.

▶ Diamond-tipped saws can cut through thick slabs of hard granite.

DIAMOND EYE

Certain surgical **scalpels** have blades made from diamonds. These are used for the most delicate surgeries, including eye surgeries.

▶ A surgeon using a diamond-tipped scalpel

RUBY LASERS

The ruby laser is the world's first working laser. It was first developed in the 1960s. The laser uses a ruby crystal to create a narrow, deep red beam of very bright light. Ruby lasers are used in medicine to help with delicate surgeries. They are also used in some laboratories to create **holograms**. In industry, ruby lasers are being replaced with other lasers. Ruby lasers are mainly used to drill holes through hard diamonds.

▲ *A laser is a device used to create a narrow, intense beam of very bright light.*

USING QUARTZ CRYSTALS

Quartz crystals are used in electronics. They can change a mechanical force into electrical energy. Quartz crystal slices are also used to regulate time in a quartz watch.

▼ *Quartz watches are very accurate.*

MOHS HARDNESS SCALE

A mineralogist named Friedrich Mohs (1773-1839) devised a scale of hardness by which all minerals can be measured. He selected ten minerals as standards and arranged them in order of hardness. Any given mineral can scratch only those minerals below it on the scale.

The softest!   *The hardest!*

1	2	3	4	5	6	7	8	9	10
talc	gypsum	calcite	fluorite	apatite	feldspar	quartz	topaz	corundum	diamond

CRYSTAL CAVES

The Cueva de los Cristales (Cave of Crystals) in Mexico contains some of the world's largest known natural crystals. The cave contains beams of gypsum crystals that are up to 36 feet (11 m) long and weigh up to 55 tons (50 metric tons).

CAVE OF CRYSTALS

The Cave of Crystals is buried 1,000 feet (305 m) below Naica Mountain in the Chihuahuan Desert. It was discovered in 2000 by two miners **excavating** a new tunnel for the Industrias Peñoles, a large mining company.

▲ Giant selenite crystals in the Cave of Crystals are the largest natural crystals ever found.

▼ Scientists work hard researching the giant crystals in Naica Mountain caves.

HOT UNDERGROUND

The cave was filled with mineral-rich water at a high temperature—around 136°F (58°C) for a very long time. At this temperature calcium and sulfate in the water reached a concentration where gypsum crystals could form. With time and slow growth, the gypsum crystals in the Naica cave could grow to their huge size.

SHINY SWORDS

In 1910, miners discovered the first crystal cave beneath Naica Mountain called the Cave of Swords. Its name comes from the crystal "daggers" that are on its walls. The Cave of Swords is close to the surface, at a depth of just 400 feet (120 m).

▼ *The Cave of Swords contains gypsum crystals that are about three feet (one m) long.*

CRYSTAL WATERS

❋ There are crystal caves in many other parts of the world including Bermuda, California, Lebanon, Canada, and Norway. Calcite and aragonite commonly form in caves as cave rock, and as crystals. The Crystal Cave in Bermuda was discovered in the 1880s.

▼ *The Crystal Cave in Bermuda has many stalactites, stalagmites, and deep crystal-clear pools.*

▼ *Ice crystals in a cave in Norway, look like tiny white Christmas trees hanging upside down.*

GEMS AND GEMSTONES

A gemstone is a mineral, rock, or **organic** material that is used for jewelry and ornaments. Rubies, pearls, and opals are types of gemstones. A gem is a gemstone that has been cut and polished to reveal its beauty. Pearls may be used to make jewelry without being cut or polished. They are gemstones, but not gems.

HEY PAL!

Opal is the most colorful gem. Fine examples can even be more valuable than diamonds. The color of opals changes with the angle at which the stone is viewed. This is called **opalescence**. The play of color may consist of large, individual flashes of color or may be of tiny, dense flashes. Opal is not a true mineral. It is called a mineraloid because it does not form crystals.

▲ *Opals displaying play of color are known as precious opals.*

BLACK LIGHTNING

Black opal is the most valuable form of opal. The most beautiful black opal comes from Lightning Ridge in New South Wales, Australia.

▶ *Black opals shine in many colors.*

PEARLY WHITE

Pearls have always been highly valued as gemstones because of their beauty. Unlike most other gemstones, which are minerals, pearls are formed organically and are created by living organisms. They are formed by the soft tissue layer of mollusks such as oysters and mussels.

▲ Gemstones, like the ruby above, have to be cut and polished to look beautiful.

▲ Almost all pearls used to make jewelry are cultured pearls. Cultured pearls are produced by inserting a small sand grain or piece of shell in the body of an oyster or mussel. An oyster or mussel then grows a pearl around the object.

▼ Ornamental figures, especially animals and religious figures, are often carved from jade.

GREEN BEAUTY

Jade is a gemstone that can be cut and polished from two minerals: nephrite and jadeite. Both minerals form in metamorphic rocks at a high temperature and under high pressure. Jade has been an important gemstone throughout history, especially in China and Latin America.

▼ Coober Pedy, a mining town in Australia, is sometimes called the "opal capital of the world" because of the quantity of opals that are mined there.

OTHER CRYSTALS

There are many other crystals that can be cut and polished into gems. Beauty, rarity, and durability are some of the qualities that make a gemstone valuable.

TOPAZ FROM BRAZIL

Topaz is a silicate mineral of aluminum and fluorine and is very hard. Topaz deposits are found all over the world in silicic volcanic rocks and pegmatites. The most beautiful topaz crystals come from the Ouro Preto area in Brazil.

▲ Most natural topaz crystals are colorless.

GREAT GARNET

Garnet can be colorless, black, or many shades of red and green depending on its chemical composition. Gemstone-quality garnet is found in several countries including the United States, the Czech Republic, Slovakia, South Africa, Australia, Brazil, and Sri Lanka. Long ago, people who were in mourning wore black garnet as jewelry.

▼ Black garnet has a deep glossy black color due to the titanium present in the stone.

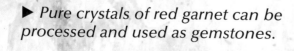

▶ Pure crystals of red garnet can be processed and used as gemstones.

TRICKY TOURMALINE

Like corundum, tourmaline is pleochroic. Tourmaline has one of the widest color ranges of any gemstone. Some crystals are even more than one color! For example, watermelon tourmaline is pink in the core and green at the outer edges, just like the fruit.

▲ Two large watermelon tourmaline crystals—the damage on one exposes the pink core

▲ Moonstones display a mysterious glow effect. This effect is caused by the special structure of its crystal formation.

MYSTERIOUS MOONSTONE

Moonstone is a form of feldspar that owes its name to its mysterious shimmer when the stone is rotated. Most moonstones are colorless with a silver or blue sheen, but some types may be steely gray, pink, yellow, orange, or pale green, and they may even change color depending on how they are viewed.

TAKE A LOOK!

Look for rocks in your backyard, a park, empty parking lots, or near a beach, and use a magnifying glass to look for crystals. You will also find white, black, and other colors of crystals in sand and gravel. There are often crystals of many different colors, sizes, and shapes in sand.

▶ Look for crystals with a magnifying glass.

BIRTHSTONE FUN

A birthstone is a gem or a gemstone that is associated with certain months of the year. Some people believe that they bring special qualities and personality traits to the people born in that month.

JANUARY—GARNET

Garnet brings happiness, wealth, and blessings. It is said to open the heart and boost self-confidence.

FEBRUARY—AMETHYST

Amethyst is associated with clearing the mind of negative thoughts and instilling courage.

MARCH—AQUAMARINE

Aquamarine is for people who love the ocean. It is associated with speaking the truth and releasing emotions.

APRIL—DIAMOND

Diamond strengthens the body and soul and symbolizes wisdom, purity, and clarity.

MAY—EMERALD

Emerald encourages positive thinking and helps with stress management. It also allows people to live up to their full potential.

JUNE—PEARL

Pearls have been popular for thousands of years because of their beauty. A pearl is very precious, as are the people born in this month.

JULY—RUBY

Ruby was considered a stone of power and royalty for a long time and by many cultures. It is believed to promote energy, balance, and to increase motivation.

AUGUST—PERIDOT

Peridot promotes friendship. It is also said to help ward off depression, envy, and fear.

SEPTEMBER—SAPPHIRE

Sapphire is known as the stone of prosperity. It relaxes and clears the mind, and increases motivation and passion for life.

OCTOBER—OPAL

Opal sharpens the mind. It encourages spontaneous and impulsive behavior, but also protects people from danger.

NOVEMBER—TOPAZ

Topaz encourages truth and honesty. It is recognized for its ability to grant us the power to control our lives.

DECEMBER—TURQUOISE

Turquoise provides overall health and strength. It balances mood swings and provides endurance and self-confidence.

GLOSSARY

abrasives Substances used for grinding, smoothing, or polishing

atoms Tiny particles that are too small for people to see. All matter on Earth is made up of atoms.

ceramics Substances, such as porcelain or brick, made by heating minerals to high temperatures

cleave To join together firmly

crust The outer layer of Earth

durability Ability to last a long time

excavating Make a hole by digging

faces Flat surfaces on the sides of crystals

gem A gemstone that has been cut and polished to reveal its beauty

gemstone A mineral, rock, or organic material that is used for jewelry and ornaments

glacial ice The ice that makes up glaciers

hologram An image formed by light beams from a laser or other light source

lava Melted rock that comes from a volcano

lustrous Describing shine or sheen especially from reflected light

magma Molten, or liquid, rock inside Earth

mantle The layer of Earth between the crust and the core

marble A metamorphic limestone

mineral A naturally occurring solid with a characteristic chemical composition and atomic structure

molecules Two or more atoms held together by chemical bonds

opalescence The quality of changing colors at different angles and light

opaque Does not let light through

organic Formed by living things

pleochroic minerals A mineral that appears to be different colors when observed at different angles

scalpel A small, sharp thin-bladed knife used by doctors

sediment Naturally occurring material that was formed by the breaking down of rocks and is transported by water

symmetry Close in size, shape, and relative position of parts on opposite sides of a dividing line or around a central point

tectonic plates Massive slabs of moving rock in the crust of Earth

MORE INFORMATION

FURTHER READING

Crystals and Gems.
R. F. Symes and R.R. Harding. DK CHILDREN. 2007.

Crystals and Gemstones.
Chris Pellant and Helen Pellant. Gareth Stevens Publishing. 2008.

Diamonds and Gemstones.
Ron Edwards and Lisa Dickie. Crabtree Publishing Company. 2004.

Minerals.
Adrianna Morganelli. Crabtree Publishing Company. 2004.

Gemstones.
Ann O. Squire. Children's Press CT. 2002.

Gemstones (DK Pockets).
Emma Foa. DK CHILDREN. 2003.

Gemstones.
Connor Dayton. PowerKids Press. 2007.

WEBSITES

How Rocks and Minerals Are Formed
www.rocksforkids.com/RFK/howrocks.html

Geology for Kids
www.kidsgeo.com/geology-for-kids/

All About Rocks
www.bestcrystals.com/kids.html

Minerals and Gems
http://science.nationalgeographic.com/science/earth/inside-the-earth/minerals-gems/

RocksForKids
www.rocksforkids.com/

INDEX